BRUSH DRAWING

AS APPLIED TO

Natural Forms and Common Objects

BRUSH DRAWING

AS APPLIED TO

Natural Forms and Common Objects

by

May Mallam

YESTERDAY'S CLASSICS
ITHACA, NEW YORK

This edition, first published in 2018 by Yesterday's Classics, an imprint of Yesterday's Classics, LLC, is an unabridged republication of the text originally published by George Philip & Son, Ltd. in 1905. For the complete listing of the books that are published by Yesterday's Classics, please visit www.yesterdaysclassics.com. Yesterday's Classics is the publishing arm of the Baldwin Online Children's Literature Project which presents the complete text of hundreds of classic books for children at www.mainlesson.com.

ISBN: 978-1-63334-105-0

Yesterday's Classics, LLC
PO Box 339
Ithaca, NY 14851

BRUSHWORK

To learn Brushwork is to learn to draw with a brush instead of a pencil—in mass instead of in outline. It has been found that children like this method, and find it easy: proportions are more readily grasped, faults are more easily seen in the filled surface, while even the work of a beginner often shows the grace and the spirit of the model. In its first stages Brushwork aims (1) at mastery of the brush; (2) at the use of the brush to draw with. In its later stages it teaches the expression of solid form by means of light and shade, and simple colouring—the beginnings of water-colour painting. Its chief object is to teach bold, simple work; it deals with general effect rather than detail; it is suggestive rather than exact. Much must be left out in using this method, but a wise "leaving out" is one of the secrets of an artist. The pupil is taught to look for the broad effects that mark the modelling, disregarding, for the time, small changes of surface and colour. When the power of doing this has been obtained, a great step has been made, and the pupil will be ready to attack more serious work.

GENERAL DIRECTIONS

Requisites—Paper fairly thick and not too smooth. A good cartridge paper for the purpose can be obtained at 1s. 1d. per quire, extra thick.

One or more hollowed palettes to hold colour: they must be able to hold quite a teaspoonful of mixed paint.

A sloping surface for the paper, to ensure the smooth run of the colour; the slope of the school desk will do, but a steeper slope is better.

Brushes not too fine: Numbers 6 or 7 are good.

Blotting paper or duster to wipe and clean the brushes.

A white screen in front of the pupil, *i.e.*, a piece of white cardboard, with a hinged stand, which can be easily made, and a couple of skewers piercing the screen, so that their rings support the specimen to be studied.

For monochrome, a tube or pan of indigo, sepia, or other suitable colour.

PLATE I

Mix your colour not too thick, but thick enough to give decided effect; fill your brush, but not so full that the paint drops from it. The drawings shew the method of holding the brush:— (1) for vertical, (2) for horizontal strokes. In every case the brush must be held parallel to the stroke to be formed. The hand should not rest on the paper, but be raised from beyond the wrist; the little finger may touch the paper to steady the hand if necessary, but the further back the weight is thrown, and the higher the hand is raised, the greater the flexibility attainable. The whole hand should be able to move to continue a long line, or to change smoothly and easily the position of the brush in a curve.

Practice all the varieties of vertical and horizontal lines till they can be done with ease. The length can be done without moving the wrist. Start by placing the brush firmly on the paper, as far forward as the fingers can reach it (the stick of the brush pointing straight downwards for the vertical, straight along for the horizontal), and pull the brush in the direction needed, letting it press out wide on the paper for the broad parts, rise to a point for the thin ones. Pay great attention to evenness of line, avoiding jags, but let the paint thicken where it happens to do so. The strokes widening on one side only are the most difficult: the hairs must be pressed to one side, while the brush is still drawn in a straight line. Then practice all the same strokes in longer lines, letting the wrist move, and also in slanting lines in any direction, starting sometimes from the top, sometimes from the bottom. It is useful to group the strokes into radiating patterns, and to insist on all the strokes being worked *to* the centre or *from* the centre. Working simple patterns is excellent training for the eye: distances must be guessed, and working out the patterns will shew how far the guess was correct. Pupils should be encouraged to make their own grouping, it makes the work more interesting, and soon leads to efforts at design. A few patterns are suggested of straight lines only—they should be much enlarged and varied. Such patterns can be invented by the dozen, or can be found on printed pamphlets, wall papers, table linen, &c. Printed letters of the alphabet make some good straight line practice. A line too long to be done in one movement should be neatly joined when the hand has taken a fresh position.

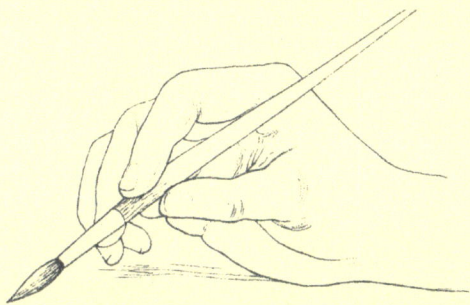

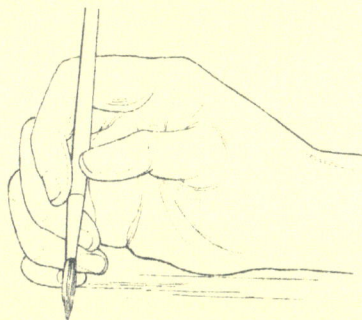

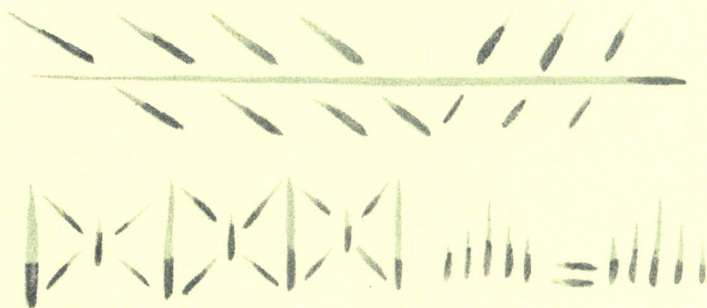

PLATE I

PLATE II

A curved line is almost more natural to the hand than a straight line, but a great deal of practice is required before the student can curve his line as he wishes every time. Hold the brush loosely and raise the hand well on the forearm so that great flexibility is possible. The direction of the brush handle will need to be constantly and smoothly changed, a twist of the brush *in* the fingers often helps to keep the hairs following the stick in a curve, and thus avoids jags. It is well to do the strokes in pairs, reversing each, and forming gradually more complicated groupings. Work from memory as much as possible, grasping the whole form of the stroke and not looking a second time at the copy. Work as a rule from top to bottom and from left to right, but vary the work for practice, only be sure always that the stick leads, the brush follows. Writing letters make good practice, and flourishes may be encouraged. The student should persevere with exercise work till he can lead his brush in fine line anywhere and make his stroke thick or thin at will. Here again pattern making is of great advantage, and becomes very fascinating. Any strokes repeated at regular intervals make a pattern or the basis of one. Dots are made with the tip of the brush, starting with a point and working round it; placed at even distances apart they will make a basis for a number of border patterns. Good work may be done too by drawing simple forms of chairs, tables, scissors, and other common objects, outlines of leaves, &c., but such work would be best done from memory, the shape being first learned. This is good training for the eye, and it enables the whole attention to be given to the management of the brush.

PLATE II

FILLED SPACES—PLATE III

The previous practice only enabled the student to work such shapes and lines as the breadth of the brush would cover; it was invaluable as training, but was directly of use chiefly in design. Work from nature or natural objects introduces at once shapes that the brush cannot fill with one movement, and here a great deal of freedom in the use of the brush must be allowed. The main object is to draw correctly, and as directly as possible, and very few rules are needed as to method.

Begin at the top of the shape to be formed, having your board sloped as advised at the beginning of this work, and, putting plenty of paint on the paper, keep it flowing downwards, shaping your mass as you proceed. Do not outline your object and fill in afterwards, this always leaves a hard edge and loses the great advantage of brushwork, *i.e.*, the drawing in solid mass. The paint must not be mixed too thick or it will not run smooth, and though, for the running, a good deal of paint must be kept on the paper, if you have too much it will be ungovernable. Let the brush rest broadly on the paper and try to get the shape you want with the first movement, though a little correction by addition is always possible.

Between different objects, or parts of an object, wherever an outline is needed other than the outer edge, leave a little line of white. These lines may be also used sometimes as veins in a leaf, stamens of a flower, or to mark a folded surface; they need to be well chosen, not too many of them, or the effect is lost, their width may be varied to make them conspicuous or otherwise as necessary. The dark and light parts in simple monochrome are accidental and should be left so, it makes a variety in the work, but if too big a blot comes in any part it should be taken up with a half dry brush, otherwise it will dry patchy.

Work from nature and solid objects is far more valuable than from copies. The present work only gives a few examples of what may be done, and every student should try to use the same methods in doing original work. Teachers may find it difficult to provide models for their classes all the year round, especially in towns, but everywhere there is something to be found, feathers, shells, insects, the contents of a workbox or tool chest, penny toys, even artificial flowers may be used in monochrome work if the shapes are good. In this work too great exactness should not be insisted on—proportions should be well kept and the spirit of the original caught, but absolutely correct work with the brush is impossible to beginners, and perhaps trying to get it will take out all the grace and spirit which

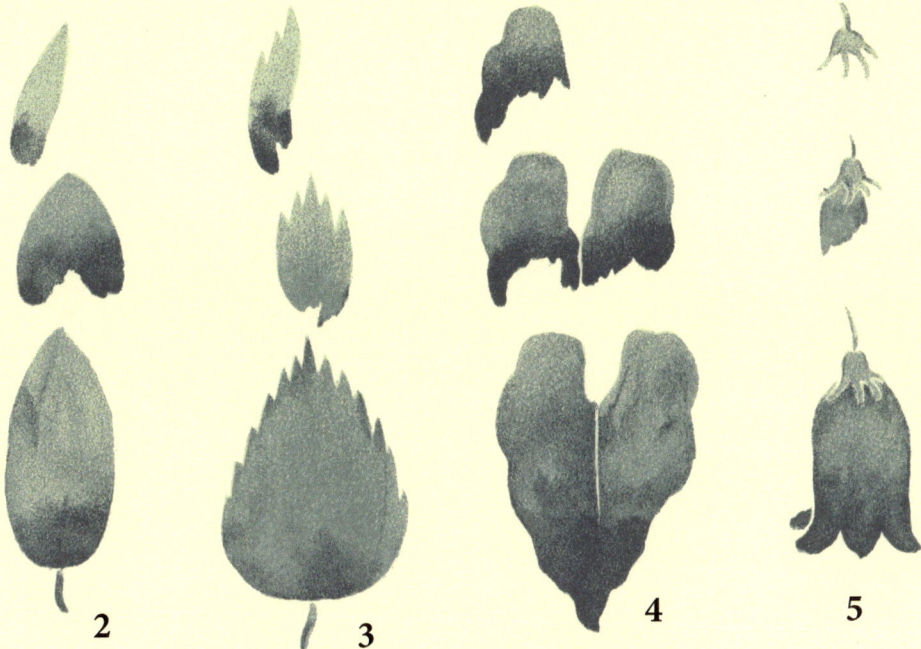

1

2

3

4

5

7

9

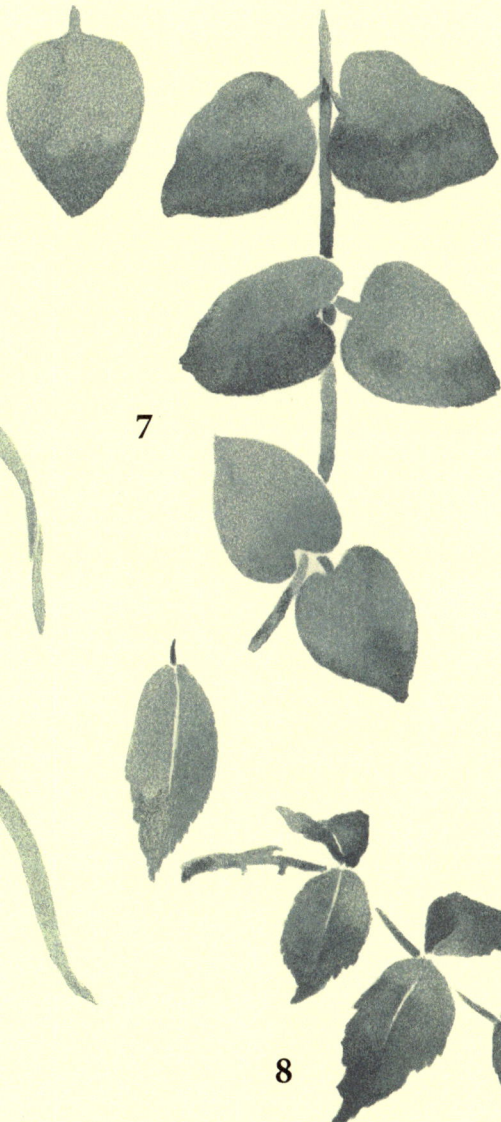

6

8

PLATE III

the student would show if left a little more free. Work from memory should be encouraged always. The teacher should examine the model with the student before he begins his work, pointing out proportions, habit of growth, &c., then any student who can, or cares to attempt it, should work from memory. A certain amount of composition is required in working from nature, the specimen must be well chosen, well placed, well balanced. If the leaves or flowers are crowded some may be cut off, and those left should be thrown up against the white screen as much as possible, not allowed to come one in front of another.

In (1) begin by a horizontal stroke for the top of the square, work below it with downward strokes and finish with another horizontal one.

(2) Two broad sweeps of the brush will nearly complete the leaf, shape the bottom carefully and let the stalk not quite touch.

(3) The jags at the top are only so many beginnings, the tip of the brush making each jag, and the colour being brought well down towards the stalk each time, start with the highest point and shape the bottom last.

(4) Bring the left half well down and leave it *wet*, then work the right down to the same level with the white line between, then let the two run together and shape the point.

(5) Draw the calyx first, then the bell, not letting it quite touch the calyx.

The grass (6) should be worked with simple brush strokes, leaving the tiny white line to mark joints and bendings of the blade.

(7) Shews a leaf (periwinkle) taken first singly and flat, then on its stalk with others, and to a certain extent in perspective. Plan out the stalk first with tiny touches, but do not put it in till the leaves are placed.

(8) The same treatment of a rose leaf, the two leaves turning back are much fore-shortened.

(9) The convolvulus leaf not much altered by its position.

1

2

3

4

5

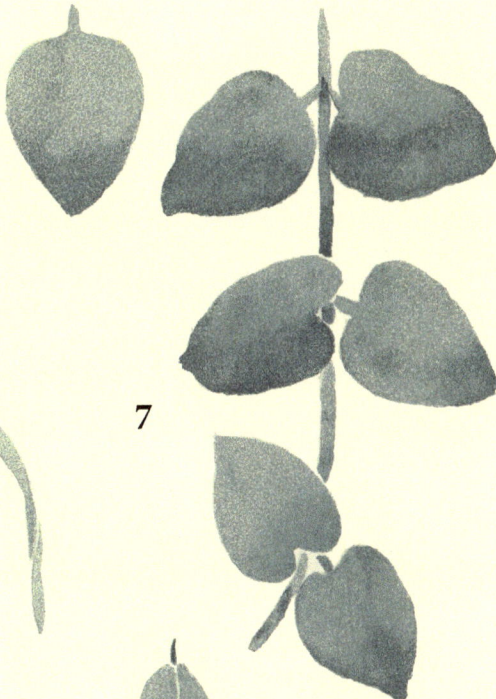
7

9

6

8

PLATE III

PLATE IV

The difficulty of drawing is lessened if the model is well examined and understood. For this purpose it is well to draw first from detached specimens, then from the group or branch, as shown on Plate IV.

The creeping buttercup (1) has five petals (2), its sepals turned upwards (3), much branched lower leaves (4).

In (2) the stamens may be worked first and the petals grouped round. In the other examples place the sepals and fit in the petals above.

The geranium (5) has five petals, two of which stand rather apart from the others.

In the blackberry (6) copy the stamens first and group the petals round, two being partly hidden, the little sepals hang down between the petals. A coloured specimen is shown on Plate XVIII.

The fuchsia (7) has shapes well adapted for brush strokes.

PLATE IV

PLATE V

Sweet Pea (1), Coreopsis (2), Potato Flower (3), and Cornflower (4). See Plate XVIII.

The coreopsis is shewn in outline to give expression to the ring of brown at the base of the petals. Notice the silhouette of the potato flower, a little arrangement will effect this without losing the clustered character of the plant.

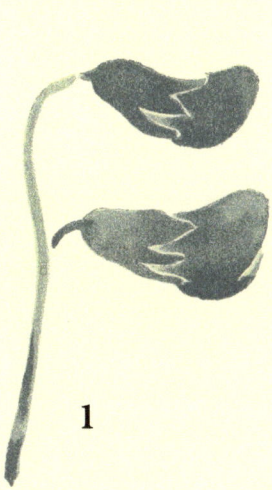

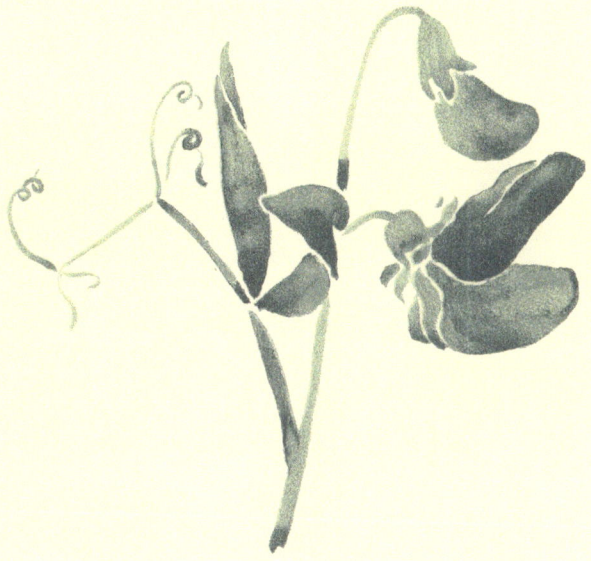

1

2

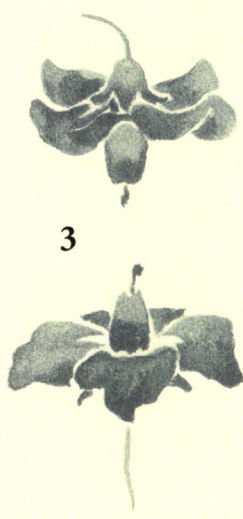

3

4

PLATE V

SHADED MONOCHROME—
PLATE VI

An advance on simple monochrome is the monochrome which shews the roundness of the object by taking note of light and shade. It is an advance towards dealing with colour, and it is a useful intermediary, as it accustoms the pupil to further examination of his model and gives him skill in dealing with more than one wash of colour. Very pretty useful work can be done at this stage.

Mix two pans of colour, one distinctly darker than the other, but not too thick, and keep a separate brush for each. The variety of colour is to be used chiefly to show shadow and therefore form, but it is possible sometimes, as in "Love in a Mist" (Plate XIX), to take note also of different tones of colour, keeping, in this case, the petals of the flower very pale, the foliage dark. The two colours may be laid side by side with a tiny white line between to prevent mixing, if the distinction of colour is very sharp—this is shewn in Numbers 1, 4, and 5; but more often the change will be gradual, and then, being laid on side by side (as in 2, 3, and 6), or in succession one above the other (as on the right hand side of 9, three of the leaflets of 11, and in the grass forms), their edges must overlap, and, both being wet, the paint will run together and make the change gradual. To keep good distinction of tone in this method the paint must not be put on too wet, and yet it must be wet enough to run smooth. Accidental variety of colour must be avoided in "Shaded Monochrome;" any run of paint to the bottom of the coloured surface must be taken up with a clean damp brush. To make a very decided light, a clean, wet paint brush may take the place of one filled with paint; this has been done in examples 7, 8, and 10. The grass and oats (12 and 13) present no difficulty: any ribbon-like foliage is excellent practice in brushwork, needing and forming a firm, free stroke. It will be seen that a white line division marks a difference of surface, a bend over of the blade (it can be seen again in the pear leaves (14)), while a gradual change is made in the way explained above. In 14, notice how the leaves have been grouped so as to be shewn in silhouette; if one part has to cross another as in 15, always work the front one, *i.e.*, the one you can see the whole of, first, and piece in the other behind, using less detail. Sharp lights and shades and much detail bring an object forward, flatter treatment throws it back.

PLATE VI

SHADED MONOCHROME— PLATE VI

(continued)

The whole effect should be obtained in one painting (one wetting of the surface), but sometimes fine markings may be added when the first colour is nearly dry; this should be avoided as much as possible. If a fault in colour needs to be corrected by a second wash, take care to wet the whole surface again slightly, with water where the extra colour is not needed; such correction must not be attempted till the first wash is quite dry. Washing out should not be tried except sometimes in fine lines for vein marks and stamens, etc. After the drawing is complete, some of the white lines may be filled in with a little faint colour if they are too conspicuous; fill those on the shaded side rather than on the light side.

In work from nature itself, attend first to placing your model so that there is distinct light and shade shewn—in masses, rather than too much intermixed. If small lights and shades appear in the masses, disregard them for the present, and represent the light as one unbroken surface, the shade as another. This neglect of detail and grasp of mass is an important element in good brushwork. When that has been thoroughly grasped, the detail may come back into notice, but it will be in right subordination to the masses. Work first from easy leaf forms taken singly, then from several on one stem, as in 14, 15, and 16. This introduces more freedom of position and broader differences of light. Work from the largest specimens available, and on a large scale, if possible.

PLATE VI

PLATE VII

Work from models of this sort is much more difficult than from leaf and flower form, because greater exactness is necessary. It is likely, too, to be less effective, as the lack of freedom will detract from the beauty of the work, but it is a good corrective of loose handling, and gives valuable lessons of light and shade.

A model should be so placed that light comes on it from one direction only; from the left is best to avoid the shadow of the hand in working. 1, 2, 3. Notice that neither the brightest light nor the darkest shade is on the edge; this is the case in all rounded objects and is due to reflection. Start from the left side and work in the darker colour when you get to the place for it. A little management will be needed to make the joining of the two tones smooth. In the centre part of the reel, work in vertical columns from left to right. It would be well to let a pupil practise the shapes in flat monochrome before attempting the light and shade. There are bright lights on the ball and the apple which are put in with a clean wet brush, and in the onion little white lines mark the edges of the outer skin. The cast shadows look less hard if a clean damp brush is drawn along their edges while still wet. Put in the calyx of the apple after the rest is complete. 7. Start with some of the middle feathers and work in the others behind, leave a few sharp outlines. 10. Cover the light surface with paint and then draw the dark lines on it while wet. 11. Draw the strings in the light colour, leaving white lights, then add the dark touches where necessary. Work similar objects from the round and try to get the solid effect as simply as possible.

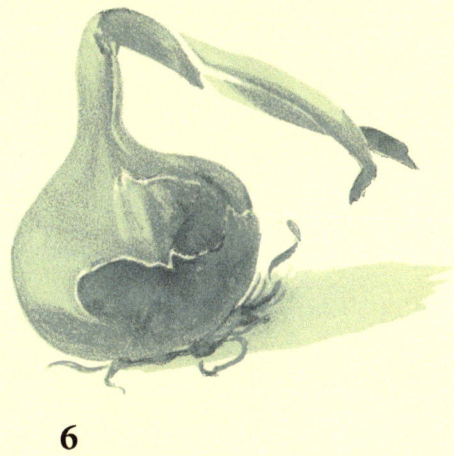

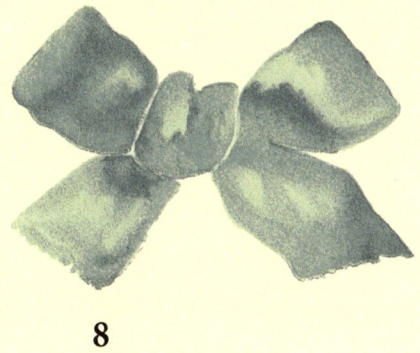

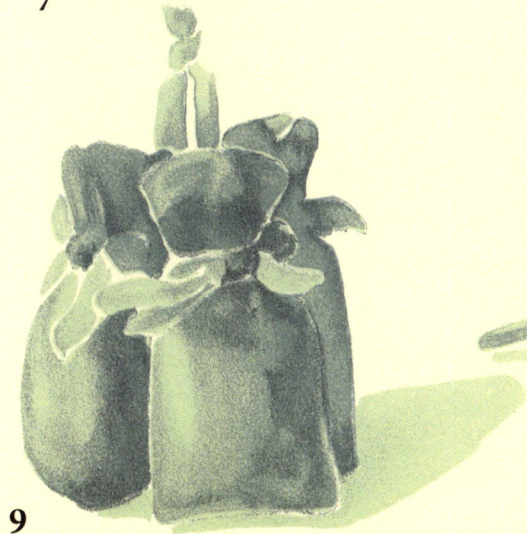

1

2

3

4

5

6

7

8

9

10

11

PLATE VII

PLATE VIII

Examples of bold treatment in the poppy heads (1) and the sunflower (2). In the sunflower, work the whole petals before those half concealed. There are two treatments of the nuts (3), the first, in simple monochrome, has the nut left quite white, which is possible because the green envelope goes all round its outline, and it is more effective so, than it would be filled up.

1

2

3

4

PLATE VIII

PLATE IX

Ivy leaves (1) treated very simply. Each leaf might be taken as a separate study before the whole is attempted. In the ivy and in the Virginia creeper (2) the vein marks are only suggested on the leaves where the surface is lightest.

1

2

PLATE IX

PLATE X

Shews treatment of a white flower, Japanese Anemone. On white paper not much can be done with white flowers. Two ways are suggested (1), (2). In the first the flower is outlined with rather a broken line and the shaded parts are painted with a light wash, the rest not touched. In the second (2) the shaded parts are painted as in 1, and the petals are completed with a clean, wet brush, carrying the tint on further and making a softer modelling. Here the study is given first in simple monochrome.

1

2

PLATE X

PLATE XI

"Love in a Mist" (1) is not as difficult as it looks. Compare it with Plate XIX. Work the upright stamens first, then the top layer of petals, leaving white lines; fill in the lower petals in a little darker colour, or begin them with a darker colour and finish them with clean water, leaving their tips not much darker than the upper petals, then work the stamens that lie over the petals and the green branching foliage. In the horned seed-vessel (2) work as in the poppy-head, but start with the five horns in dark colour. The laburnum (3) is quite simple.

1

2

3

PLATE XI

PLATE XII

The modelling of the shells is a little difficult—1 is quite straight forward work, 2 and 4 may need to have the dark inside shading strengthened after the other work has been completed, if so, it should, in 2, have the lower edges taken up with a clean, wet brush to make the new colour blend with the rest; in 4, the edges are sharp top and bottom. The grapes (3) are easy, they should be painted lightly to give some idea of transparency; 5 is fairly easy, work each division in the light colour and add markings of the darker one. In the feather (6) paint the two sides separately, leaving the quill white; a line of shadow must be added to it afterwards. Let the brush follow the direction of the side feathers with each movement, and then it will give the position of the shadow lines on the right hand side which come between two strokes of the light wash brush. Begin at the tip of the fir cone (7) and fit in the bits as shewn larger at the side; keep the shaded effect to the right. The pearly effect of the honesty (8) is got by painting the shadow in the light colour as in 9, and continuing with water as in 10; the outline may be put in in places, but to put it everywhere would be stiff.

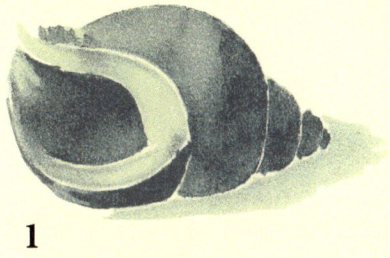

1

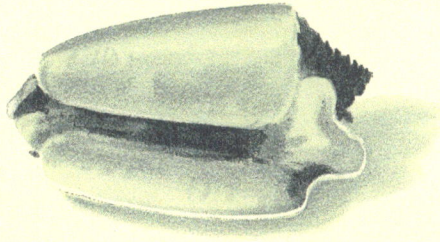

2

3

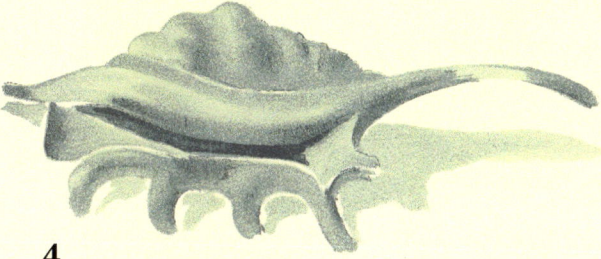

4

5

6

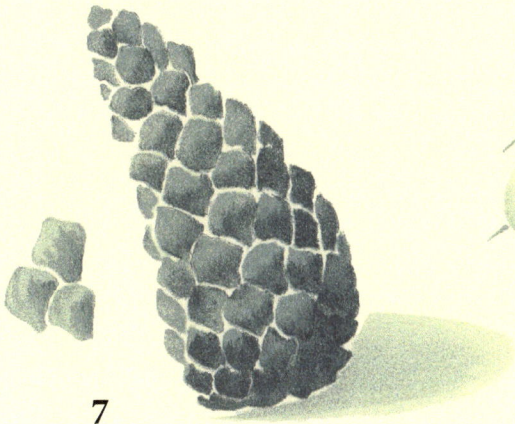

7

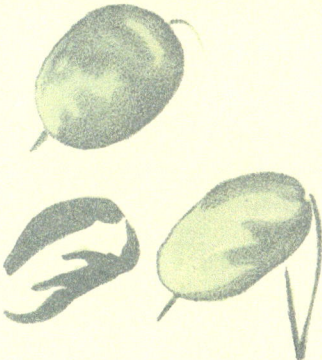

9

10

8

PLATE XII

PLATE XIII — COLOUR

The light and shade study will have led the student to examine well his model, to see endless differences of colour and of light, but to restrain his expression of them so as to work simply and boldly. All that has been said in "Shaded Monochrome" as to the method of handling two 'tones,' is applicable to this work in which more than one colour must be dealt with, and need not be repeated—one study will have done much to facilitate the other. The additional difficulties in this work are—1, the mixing of colour; 2, the right shading of each colour.

All the examples in this book have been painted with no other colour than carmine, Prussian blue, and gamboge. From these three, almost endless varieties of tint may be obtained, but with some trouble; the blues and mauves are perhaps the most difficult. Plate XIII shows some of the mixtures possible, and beside each example, afterwards is shewn a list of the colours which have been employed in it. In every case, the various colours to be used should be prepared beforehand in different compartments of a palette, that the work may go straight on; it saves time and paint to have a separate brush for each, and it is of great advantage that the sticks of the brushes should be differently marked, so as to be easily distinguishable, but if these things are impossible the brush must be washed and slightly dried on blotting paper or a rag when a fresh colour is to be used.

The choosing and well placing of a specimen is very important. Flowers of complicated form such as the rose, with delicate petals like the sweet pea and the shirley poppy, with very finely cut leaves, or of close growth, had better be avoided as subjects. You want bold treatment, and you must suit your subject to your work. Take flowers of simple and decided form, large ones if possible, with not too many stamens, and draw them, in some cases, larger than life size. Use leaf study largely: it is generally easy to obtain and is beautiful in modelling. The specimen should be placed, as already advised in General Directions, in front of a white screen if the work is to be done on white paper, which is best, and it should be arranged so as to be in silhouette, or nearly so, and to give light and shade in masses; few changes but decided ones. The examples given in this part of the work are many of them the same as were given in "Monochrome" or in "Shaded Monochrome." This is arranged purposely—it is a good plan to study the drawing of an object in monochrome before trying it in colour. The student might go back to his former work and copy on to one page the fuchsia on Plate IV, that on Plate XIII, and that on Plate XVIII; the coreopsis, potato flower, etc., in the same way, and follow the same plan in working from nature.

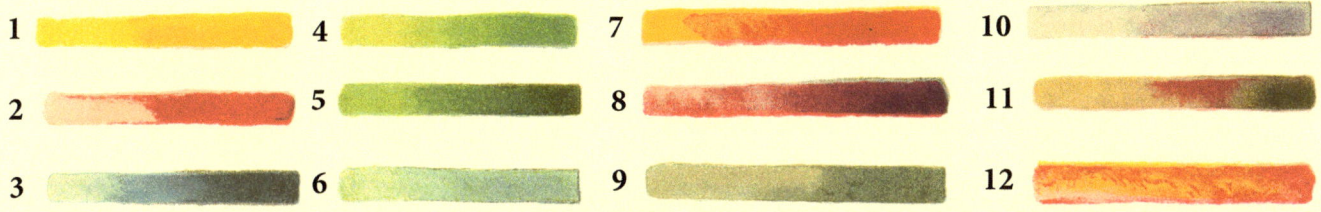

1
2
3
4
5
6
7
8
9
10
11
12

PLATE XIII

PLATE XIII — COLOUR
(continued)

Nearly all the "Common Objects" given in "Shaded Monochrome" will make good subjects for "Shaded Colour"; reels of cotton, bows of ribbon, coloured balls are especially recommended.

MIXING OF COLOUR

We all know the simple mixtures—yellow + blue = green; blue + crimson = purple; yellow + red = orange—but the mixtures of all three colours are not so familiar, and they must be largely used if the work is to represent nature with any truth—if it is to avoid crudeness and vulgarity. Three greens are shewn, 4, 5, 6, and they are needed in nearly every example: 1 is made simply of Prussian blue and gamboge; 2 has carmine in addition; 3 has a little carmine, but Prussian blue predominates; 7 and 8 are the simple mixtures mentioned above; 9 contains all three colours—no exact recipe is possible, but there is perhaps least yellow, most blue: the effect is a perfectly neutral grey, shading to black if the mixture is strong enough; 10 is Prussian blue and carmine, with a little yellow to give the greyness of mauve; 11 has all three colours, carmine and gamboge in greatest proportion to make brown; 12 is gamboge laid on alone and carmine laid over it when dry, this gives a brighter orange and scarlet than can be obtained by mixing the paints, but is apt to be spotty.

On Plate XIII also are a few examples of flowers and leaves treated with colour, but with no light and shade. This may be done for some time, to accustom the pupil to mixing and matching colour, but it does not present much more difficulty than the simple monochrome, and not many examples are therefore given.

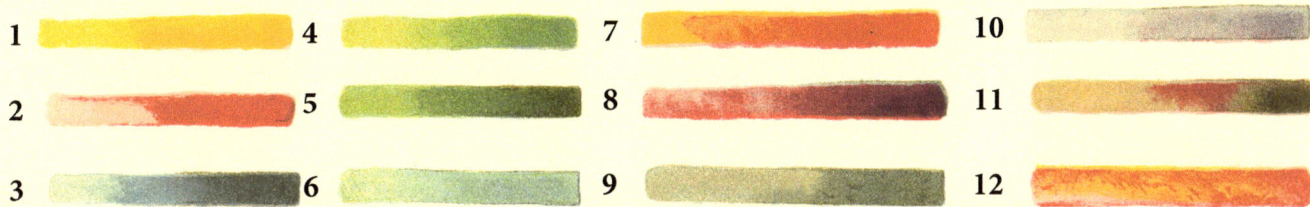

PLATE XIII

PLATE XIV

The colours used on Plate XIV are those shewn on Plate XIII, 4, 5, 6; the treatment is almost exactly that of Plate VI, but the blue green (6) replaces the clean, wet brush. In studying from foliage, the blue green (6) usually occurs where the light strikes full on a surface, the bright yellow green (4), where the light comes through the leaf and in young foliage, the darker green (5), in the parts lying in shadow; this colour may be much varied, being warmer, *i.e.*, more carmine, in examples 7 and 11 Plate XV, bluer in the ivy 1 and 2 Plate XV. The daffodil foliage has blue green (6) as its prevailing colour; this would occur also in carnation grass, tulip leaves and some of the garden poppy plants.

PLATE XIV

PLATE XV

1, 2, 3, 4, 5 and 6. The second leaf is a little more modelled than the first, they represent different degrees of attainment. In 2 the vein-mark has been added by taking up with a clean damp brush, well pointed; in 6, by covering up the white line with darker colour. It often looks well to show the vein-marks in the light part of a leaf and leave them to the imagination on the dark side. 4 has had vein marks added while the paint was still wet. In 7, notice that one leaf has been more elaborately modelled than the others; that is often a good plan in order to bring one leaf more forward, and to make the work less monotonous. In 11, try to keep the bumpy surface of the acorn cup, and the smooth surface of the acorn.

PLATE XV

PLATE XVI

This plate deals with other colours—yellow, blue, and pink, shaded. The shade on yellow must not be too strongly marked or the work will be heavy; a slight green shade gives the best effect where only the simplest treatment is possible. Sometimes in a deep yellow flower, as the bird's foot trefoil (4), the yellow should be strengthened in the shaded part before the green is added. In all the yellow flowers let the yellow go all over, and run in the green while the surface is still wet. 2 and 3 show different stages of painting the nasturtium, the dark markings being added last in that and in the pansy (1).

The shading of blue is grey or mauve. Blues and mauves are difficult with the three paints in use. Prussian blue can be used, very pale, to make a forget-me-not colour, 5, and very pale mauves are easy, but the deeper mixtures look muddy. Many of the mauves and purples can only be suggested, as in 6, by laying a blue wash and a pink wash side by side—the blue representing light, the pink, shade. The Prussian blue is made to look purer and less hard by keeping the shadows very pink, as in 7. A mixture of two colours best represents the blue crane's bill (8). The shading of pink is mauve; in the pale blues and pale pinks the ground colour has been put on all through and the shading colour added while the surface was wet, but in the darker clematis (9), the colours have been put on side by side and allowed to mix in the usual way.

PLATE XVI

PLATE XVII

A few of the flowers of Plate XVI drawn more freely and shewing their growth. The scarlet is a new colour; its two shades are the same mixture of carmine and gamboge used in different depths. The treatment is absolutely simple, but it gives a good idea of what is really a most difficult subject, and thus fulfils the aims of brushwork. In the nasturtium leaf the colour is put on all over with its varying tint as shewn, and the vein marks are taken out afterwards with the tip of a damp brush. If lines are to shew sharply, as in the bud of the clematis (1) and the calyx of the campion (3), they should be added on a nearly dry surface.

1

2

3

4

PLATE XVII

PLATE XVIII

Compare with Plates IV and V, where the shapes have been already practised. Notice how the red colour goes all through the fuchsia, appearing in the stems and the shadow of the green ovary. The coreopsis is most easily worked from the outside—the yellow can go far in and the brown be put on over it. Slender foliage like that of the coreopsis can often be worked in one green only. The mauve of the potato flower is done in one mixture, but the paint is left thicker in parts. The painting of the single flower should be a little more elaborate than that of the grouped or growing one; more freedom can be used if there are other parts to explain and add to the work. In flowers with feathery stamens as the blackberry blossom, work the stamens first and the petals round them.

Fuchsia

Coreopsis

Potato Flower

Blackberry

PLATE XVIII

PLATE XIX

The corn cockle is one of the reddish mauves difficult to represent, but it is given for the sake of its simple and beautiful form. Finish the three upper red petals with water before proceeding to the grey shadow inside the flower. The flower and seed vessel of "Love in a Mist" can be completed as shewn, before the spiky foliage is added. The method of work has been explained for Plate XI.

Corn Cockle

Love in a Mist

Laburnum

PLATE XIX

PLATE XX

Feathers are rather difficult. The passing from one colour to another is often sudden and distinct, but not hard; this effect will be produced if the paint is not too wet. In 1 and 3, half the feather can be worked before the other half is touched, and a distinct white line left for the quill, which can be afterwards filled up. In 2, the two sides are alike, and had better be worked at the same time. Keep the succession of colours, working according to the formation of the feather, and let the colours run together; in the lower part, lay yellow on first and let the green not quite cover it. 7, 8, and 9 are very simple in treatment; 4, 5, and 10 are a little more elaborate than anything else in the book, the painting cannot be completed all at once. In 4 and 5, begin with the body; in 5, begin the wings by placing the black and blue patches, and fill up round them. In 10, begin with the light patches, fitting one into another, and then fill up between; notice the shadow on the right.

Wild Duck

1

2

Parrot

3

Orange Tip

4

Tiger Moth

5

Virginia Creeper

Fowl

6

9

Radish

7

Carrot

8

Fir Cone

10

PLATE XX

www.ingramcontent.com/pod-product-compliance
Lightning Source LLC
Chambersburg PA
CBHW061056090426
42742CB00002B/65